Now I Know

Bears

Written by Susan Kuchalla
Illustrated by Kathie Kelleher

Troll Associates

Library of Congress Cataloging in Publication Data

Kuchalla, Susan.
  Bears.

   (Now I know)
   Summary: Brief text and pictures portray the
characteristics and habits of bears.
   1. Bears—Juvenile literature. [1. Bears]
I. Kelleher, Kathie, ill. II. Title.
QL737.C27K82   599.74′446   81-11368
ISBN 0-89375-674-1   AACR2
ISBN 0-89375-675-X (pbk.)

10   9   8   7   6   5   4

Bears are powerful animals.

Bears walk on all four legs.

But sometimes they stand up on two legs.

Most bears live where it is cold.
Their fur keeps them warm.

Some bears have very large bodies.
This is a big grizzly bear.

SPECTACLED BEAR

POLAR BEAR

SLOTH BEAR

BROWN BEAR

But the biggest bear of all is the brown bear.

The brown bear likes to eat fish.

Which bear has a white coat?
The polar bear does.

It is hard to see polar bears in the snow.

The smallest bear is called the sun bear.
It likes to climb trees.

All bears eat a lot in the summer.

They get big and fat.

In the winter, they do not eat!

They sleep all winter in caves or hollow logs.

But sometimes, a bear wakes up and looks outside.

If it is not too cold, he may go out and look for a
winter snack!

In the spring, baby bears are born.

They are very small, with very little fur.

They stay close to their mother.

But they also like to have fun!

The mother bear takes good care of her babies.

She teaches them how to find food.
They like all kinds of things to eat.

Meat, eggs, nuts, and fruit
are some of the things they like.

They also like to eat ants!

But most of all, they like honey!